Success Strategies for Relationship and Marriage

Chinelo Maryann Chibueze

DEDICATION

This work is dedicated to all persons facing emotional challenges in their life and marriage.

ACKNOWLEDGEMENTS

My undiluted appreciation goes to my darling husband for his support, care, and motivation to see that this book becomes a reality.

I sincerely appreciate my good friend, Sir Nso Cyprain, for his care and support towards the success of this project. May the Almighty God bless you abundantly. I also appreciate my uncle Okechukwu Anene for his kind advise, moral support and encouragement towards the success of this work.

This book is the outcome of my recognition of God's call upon my life on relationship and marriage.

I give special thanks to my lovely sister and caring brother and all my sisters and brothers-in-law for their financial and spiritual support and encouragement towards my vision, dream, and life. I pray that God will continue to uphold and support you in all your endeavors.

Moreover, I want to use this medium to show appreciation to all my friends and everyone – men, women, young, and old – who I cannot name but have, in one way or the other, contributed morally, financially, prayerfully towards the success of this project. I appreciate everything you have done for me. May the Almighty God bless you all abundantly.

Lastly, I return all the glory on this project back to God, who carried me through my relationship and helped me settle down comfortably with my soul mate. I'm truly enjoying the ride. Father, I thank you.

TABLE OF CONTENTS

INTRODUCTION

Marriage is an institution established by God.

In the book of Genesis1:20, God recognized that Adam had a problem of loneliness and provided him the perfect solution – a woman to be his wife. God, who remains the source of every perfect gift (James1:17), knew just how to form a woman.

God's true purpose in establishing marriage is for one to have a helpmeet, multiply, and fulfill their God- ordained purpose on earth.

Marriage is a sacred relationship and also a lifetime commitment. I advise you to take your time while choosing a life partner and not to compare yourself with anyone else.

Marriage is an honorable institution, called so and made so by God Himself. That is another area in this book where God's mind, by His grace, is clarified.

Success Strategies in Relationship and Marriage is considered a study book. It's a guide for singles to recognize some essential points that will expose their minds to building a healthy relationship that will lead to marriage.

To the married, this book is an eye-opener. It helps couples understand and realize the necessary steps to take.

CHAPTER ONE

LOVE YOURSELF ENOUGH, TO BE ABLE TO LOVE SOMEONE ELSE

Some years ago, there was this friend of mine who didn't like to associate with anybody. Even her family members complained bitterly about her unwillingness to disclose any of her issues. We became friends by sheer coincidence.

I watched her life closely and decided to engage in a deep conversation with her. Many times, I had tried, but it was a bit difficult as she would always shy away from it. Later, I was able to convince her. I did so through my lifestyle to invest some level of trust in me, and she was glad she did. She began to gain so much confidence in me to the extent that she entrusted me with her life. After quite a short while, she opened up to me regarding her reasons for living an estranged life.

“I decided to avoid people because I realized that they do not like me and do not want to associate with me,” she began, “thus, whenever I force myself emotionally on them, they usually make me an object of laughter and mockery.”

I didn't know what to say yet, so I just nodded as she went on.

“Some say I’m big and dirty; others say I do not look attractive," she concluded.

"To what extent do you love yourself?” I asked in return.

She became quiet, looking a bit perplexed by my question. The question seemed to remain surprising to her until I clarified it to her on the basis that she needed to establish love within her first before she could talk about loving someone else or expecting love from other people.

“Personal development is the key to finding true love,” I emphasized, “personal development is essential as regards relationship and every other area of life.”

My friend and I then journeyed on the need for reflection. I led her to reflect on her life. So she was able to point out the areas where she was not doing too well. Some of the results of this reflection are exposed below.

To begin with, it turned out she was a dirty type as she could comfortably stay without properly washing her used clothes or taking a proper bath daily.

Her next area of weakness was her food addiction. She had

little or no control over anything edible. She could not control her excessive craving for food to the extent that she might even wake up at about 1:00 a.m. to eat whatever she could lay her hands.

My friend also led a lonely life because most of her friends got married while she could not yet boast of any serious relationship.

After opening up to me, things began to change for the better in my friend's life. As I taught her the need for maintaining cleanliness and getting herself in control of her life, she then began to experience a difference in everything.

She first learned neatness and practically engaged the attitude in all she did. It ranged from having a regular and proper bath to developing self-control and personal discipline, especially regarding her eating habit.

Then she took her personal development to the next level by enrolling in a paid gymnastics class to keep fit.

The result of her efforts was tremendous. Within only three months, she recorded so much positive change that people who usually spoke ill of her began to seek her attention and friendship. Now, with what my friend's experience has taught me, my success advice will come in two key points.

1. Be happy being alone

I love this saying so much: “If you are miserable by yourself, then you will be too easily offended by the first person who comes along and gives you something to do.” Matter-of-factly, being single when almost all your friends are married is not funny at all. You may want love more than anything else in the world. It is natural for you to feel lonely or even sad if you can’t find it. But part of loving yourself is to enjoy spending some time alone and finding ways to stay interested and excited about life without a significant other. You feel even happier when that "special" person eventually comes along.

What’s the bottom line of it all? “Don’t mistake companionship for love.”

2. Love yourself enough before expecting a partner

Loving yourself enough while you wait for the person who will complement you – the person with whom you will spend the rest of your life – is the easiest way to ensure that you’ll be committing yourself to that person for the right reasons. In the real sense of it, you don't need to be 100% satisfied with yourself. But if you are unhappy with your true self, then you're at risk of getting in union with someone just because they make you feel better about yourself.

Loving yourself begins with knowing who you are, and this

leads us into purpose discovery. It's so pathetic that many singles waiting for marriage are still struggling with purpose discovery. They still wander in the wilderness of confusion, seeking the best way to fulfill their destiny.

MAN'S TRUE IDENTITY

To be yourself in a world that is constantly trying to make you something else is the greatest accomplishment – Ralph Waldo Emerson –

You can trace the recognition of who you are from the origin of man. When you don't know whose child you are, anything is permitted to happen in your life; you allow people to treat you like trash with no value.

Who are you in reality?

"So God created man in His image, in the image of God He created him; male and female He created them . . ." reveals the Bible in Genesis 1: 27.

Dear you, never allow another person's view to validate who God says you are. The reasons are not far- fetched.

i. God says that He created us in His image; therefore, we are small gods. In Genesis 1:28, God gave us dominion over all the living things that move on the earth. So we are meant to be in charge and experience more of the power of God.

ii. You are a royal priesthood, a godly nation. As royalty, you are to rule your world, that is, with the understanding in the word of God. Through faith, you recreate your world. You cannot be a godly nation and allow a satanic verdict to take a position in your life. Therefore, stand tall in the word of God.

iii. God bought you with a price. 1Cor 6:20 assures us that He has paid the ultimate price for us with the stainless, spotless blood of His Son Jesus Christ. Therefore, we must glorify God in our bodies by living a sin-free life. In your quest to build a godly relationship, you must put all these into consideration.

In learning the mind of God in your relationship, it must be free from any form of filthiness. As a Christian, You can't keep asking God His will concerning a particular person while you still go ahead defiling your body with them through sexual immorality. The truth is that you may not have a sincere answer from God because he's too holy to behold iniquity.

Hey, in your relationship with someone, that person must recognize your true identity. That will enable them to relate to you according to who you are because that defines you.

Remember that for anyone whose father is a king, being a slave in his father's kingdom is an unfathomable error. Therefore, you should recognize your true identity and take advantage of it.

Know who you are and be yourself.

SEE WHO YOU ARE!

If you are going to walk in victory over Satan, you must know full well your identification with Christ, in every stage of His redemptive work.

When you know your redemptive right and positioning, you will develop and constantly carry a victory mentality. Until you know and have an understanding of who you are under your new birth, you may remain in the very bondage of Satan from which Jesus has set you free.

It becomes easy to appropriate your liberty when you know those things.

- You are translated

At salvation, you are translated into the kingdom of God, "Who hath delivered us from the power of darkness and has translated us into the kingdom of His dear Son" (Colossians 1:13).

In the kingdom of darkness, there are all forms of evil. All manners of sickness, affliction, embarrassment, torment, disappointment, marital failure, and bad luck hold sway in this kingdom of darkness. The inhabitants have no source of help for as long as they continue dwelling therein. They are ruled and governed by the devil.

The Bible calls them the children of disobedience, and the

devil continually lords it over them. They cannot protest. They have no right to. Their will has been submitted to the devil. They are servants of sin (Rom 6:16), held in bondage by the devil.

You have been brought out of darkness into light. You have become a partaker of the life and nature of the Father God (2 Peter 1: 14). God with His family is the highest class there is. This is where you now belong.

I would like you to be aware of the beauty of this translation. The essence of Christianity borders on it. Until you experience it, you remain terrestrial and everything that functions here on earth will work against you and destroy you. Marriage is not exempted. Seek to experience your translated position. It works!

You are translated into the Kingdom of light to experience:

1. Real love
2. A successful relationship that will lead to marriage;
3. Peace and harmony;
4. A blissful marriage.

- You are Peculiar

Every cleansed person is a peculiar treasure! You are not common (Acts 10:15). You're bought with a price, the precious Blood of the Lamb. You belong to royalty; you're the holiness of God, chosen to show forth the praises of

God on earth.

You are peculiar, different, and strange. You are a special breed who deserves to be envied. This is made clear in 1 Peter 2:9-10a: "But you are a chosen generation, a royal priesthood, a holy nation, a peculiar people; that ye should show forth the praises of him who hath called you out of darkness into His marvelous light. Which in time past were not a people, but are now the people of God."

As a peculiar personality, the negativity associated with relationships is not your portion because you operate from a peculiar kingdom better than the earthly. Therefore, you are destined to enjoy happiness, peace of mind, and marital security.

- You are a winner

There is an innate victory mentality in your new nature. God's son, God's daughter produced after His kind. So you're in His class. You're odd here on earth (Psalm 82: 6). By the virtue of your new birth, you have been declared a winner. You have a winning covenant with God your Father. You are no longer a victim of a wrong decision, especially in choosing a spouse, career, accommodation, business, or friend.

You can't be a winner in the Lord and fail in marriage because God guides every step you take. You are a born winner!

IMPLICATIONS OF WRONG DECISIONS

Many people take wrong decisions that will cost them greatly or expose them to harm only to regret them afterward. This is terrible. Many people who are suffering today are doing so as a result of wrong decisions taken in the past.

A young lady sought my assistance regarding her suitor. She needed me to assist her in praying for God's will in her marriage to her man. After undergoing prayer of inquiry from the Lord, the Holy Spirit confirmed the young man to be her right husband. I delivered the message unto her and she was glad.

A few months later, she told me that she wasn't interested in the marriage any longer. Before I could utter a word, she said her decision was final.

After a few months, I was surprised to notice that she had developed an interest in another man and was equally ready to marry him.

"Can we seek God's face and confirm His will as regards the said person?" I asked.

"There is no need for that," she replied.

I tried to persuade her but I sensed that there would be a great misunderstanding between us if I pressed further.

After about two years of their marriage, they separated. It was then that it dawned on her that she had taken a wrong decision, but it was too late for her. She could only regret, for there was nothing that she could muster at that point.

Mr. Lot in the Bible took a wrong decision (Gen. 13), by choosing before his uncle, Abraham, a place that he thought was the best for him. But he never knew that he had made the worst mistake of his life.

One of the little things that differentiate a person who is a good steward of time from those who waste their time is a matter of making godly decisions. That begins with the regular decisions of each day. The more biblical we are in making daily decisions, the less time we're going to waste.

If we want to avoid wasting our lives as the biblical Samson did, we must be committed to making careful, wise decisions. We need to develop good habits when it comes to making wise choices in our lives. This is because every choice comes with a set of consequences.

Below are some of the wrong decisions that Sampson took that led to his death (Judges 14:1-3):

- He went to the wrong place.
- He gave in to the lust of his eyes.
- He scorned the counsel of other people.

Many people always feel a looming death. Some behave as if

they see death as a personality around them. Some others are being controlled by evil voices to run into an oncoming vehicle or other means of committing suicide.

A young man living with a friend came back from work one day. He had worked a night shift and had just reached home when his friend, the owner of the house, was leaving for work. Nobody knew what had happened to the young man but he locked himself up and hanged himself. It was when his friend's fiancé that came and tried to get in that she discovered that the door was locked on the inside. When she looked through the window, she saw that the lifeless body of her fiancé's friend dangling from the ceiling fan hook.

For us to take the right decision, most especially in marriage, we must put God at the center of our heart and be willing to accept His choicest will for us. Wrong decisions can push someone into the feeling of looming death.

Before you consider yourself a failure, always remember that countless sperm cells contested with the one that produced you, yet the one that formed you was the only one the egg chose on purpose. At least about forty million – minus one – other sperm cells had no choice but to give way for you. So please rid your mind of those negative thoughts and do what you can with what you have wherever you are now.

Seriously, we have to stress again that loving yourself to the full before finding the person with whom you want to spend the rest of your life is the easiest way to ensure that you'll be committing yourself to that person for the right reasons.

You don't necessarily have to get 100% satisfied with yourself; however, if you're unhappy with whom you are, then you are still at risk of bonding with just anyone because you think they make you feel better about yourself. In a sense, yes, the person you get to marry "should complement you" and cause you to feel whole as a person, but this doesn't change the fact that you should already love who you are before then. Only then can you genuinely feel blessed that the person you want to be with makes you feel even better. For how long will you remain someone who constantly looks up to another person who can fill in all of the gaps in your unsatisfactory life? Always be happy with who you are, what you do, and how you look. It will not only make it easier for you to attract people through your confidence, but it will also make your life much better.

CHAPTER TWO

LOOKING FOR WHOM TO MARRY?

Know What You Want In A Partner

He brought up a topic. "I don't even know whom to marry," he said.

Sammy, as I fondly call him, had been my friend and neighbor awhile. He was young and fair-complexioned, brilliant, and diligent. He had been exposed to all manner of women right from his university days. Currently, he wanted to marry but could not find any lady worthy of a wife.

As he was sharing his experience with me, his chief complaint was that most female friends that he had were only after his money and that he couldn't point out any of them that genuinely loved him. He stressed that many of the ladies might wish to marry him not because of love but because of his financial status. He said that he had confirmed this fact by conducting several tests on different female friends of his.

"The truth is that they all failed the test," he lamented.

Hey, in your quest to marry, do not just focus on the financial capacity of the person in question. You should rather lookout for those things you desire to see in your spouse; they are the things that define him or her.

Once you can see the qualities you desire in a partner, stick to that person and enjoy a peaceful marriage. The challenge that I notice a lot of the time is that most young people usually search for the ideal man or woman. Your "ideal" husband or wife is already married; get that! That is why some people fall in love with married people.

Oftentimes, this man or that lady who looks perfect now was not like that before he or she got married. Here is the big question: if in your vision, your husband is a CEO, can you recognize him when he is not yet a CEO?

Back then when I barely knew my husband, though his financial capacity was low at the time, I saw a giant in him. I saw someone willing to do anything legitimate to make money. I loved him not just because of some personal attractions or riches but for who he was. I loved him because he had attributes that I wanted in a man; I saw a part of me in him.

From my husband's perspective, he told me that when he first saw me, even though he was attracted to me, he never allowed my beauty to deceive him. He went further to keep a healthy relationship with me, which helped him discover that I had what he had been looking for in a woman. Without much delay, he went on proposed to me regardless of his financial status.

No doubt, riches are good; fame or popularity is also good, but those things should not be the priority when choosing whom to marry. I have issues with young men who are turning bachelorhood into an institution. There are a lot of people around town who are not getting married yet because they want to first own a mansion, have some money and cars before marriage. They already have a job and they are waiting to have an ideal financial situation before marriage. Permit me to tell you that if you are in such a situation, you have been deceived.

What a lady needs is not a perfect man in the present; she needs is a man who has a vision, a man who can define exactly where he is going and who he will become. That is what also defines the kind of wife you should marry as a man.

As a man, the essence of leadership is having a vision and a capacity to communicate it. You should be able to sell your vision to a lady. As a lady, if your assessment about a man is who the person is today, you will soon be deceived because the fact that he has a car now does not guarantee that he will have a car in five years.

Choosing as regards marriage is largely a matter of intuition. All that some people think about is the wedding day. After the wedding day, what's next? Who is the person going to be? This is the reason becoming spiritually mature is critical; your spiritual maturity is the key thing. Your greatest asset in finding the right person to marry is your ability to hear from God. No one can accurately predict or tell what is going to be best for you except God.

During courtship, ensure that you understand your partner's goal. Feel free to ask him or her about his or her life, in case you don't know.

Another secret is that you should ensure that you have arguments sometimes. This is because it's during such times that you will understand your partner's true temperament and adjust yourself where necessary. Tolerance cannot be neglected in any serious relationship. You should also know your partner's friends. Go out with your partner on most occasions to meet his or her friends. This will not only make them know you in person but it will give you a wholesome sense of togetherness.

Sometimes, you both must undergo financial stress as a team. This will enable you to stand the test of time in the future alongside your partner; you both will never give up on each other. When two people are deeply committed to the success of their relationship, they face a lot of challenges together. Financial stress is not exempted.

As the scripture rightly puts it, one plus one is one in marriage, not two. The two parties must realize that the success and failure of their relationship are dependent on both of them; they win together as a team and suffer any loss together. This will fortify them to face any further challenges and come out victorious in the end.

PRACTICAL TIPS FOR CHOOSING WHOM TO MARRY

1. Be yourself

Every successful relationship begins with self-realization. You don't pretend to be what you are not. Your perfect match will love you for being you and not someone else. When you are with the person who not only accepts but embraces your quirks and flaws, you will feel loved and accepted. You will feel that you can make mistakes without judgment and explore your true self without needing to hide behind a person.

My husband and I often have astonishingly silly moments together in full expression of ourselves without any pretense. Sometimes, I would look deep into his eyes and say, "I wouldn't think of someone else who would love and understand me more than you do."

We all sometimes become different persons depending on whom we are with: family, friends, colleagues, or religious groups. Switching between different versions of you gets tiring. So you should always aim to be your true self without being forced into something you are not.

2. You both should have similar vision

Who you are now is less than where you are going. This not only applies to our lives but also greatly applies to our relationships as well. In our initial conversations, my husband and I already found that we shared a common vision. From the way we wanted to raise our kids to the lifestyles we were striving for and what each of us wanted to accomplish. At the time, we were nowhere close to any of those things, but we found comfort in the idea of working towards our goals together.

Marrying a man that will allow me access to my career had been my utmost desire when I was single. On one of the occasions when my husband and I were dating, we started a discussion about my career and academic intention. He comfortably told me that he would give me his full support as far as my career is concerned. So from his speech, I already know he would be a supportive husband.

While dating, you must pay serious attention to your vision and ensure that your partner is fully in support of it. You both should share a similar vision.

3. You both cannot blow hot at the same time

You cannot both have an uncontrollable temper; you cannot both have an issue with forgiveness. Not only will your marriage be a battle zone, but the battle extends into other areas of your lives. One of you must be willing to give in and tolerate the other.

Dear singles, if you have a partner who is supporting you to keep malice with people, a partner who breaks bottles and hands them to you when you are fighting people, or a partner who cannot calm you down at the moment of your anger, then you're in the wrong relationship.

Be with someone who has part of your weakness, someone who knows how to silence the roaring lion in you when it wants to engage in a wrong battle.

4. You don't feel ashamed around your partner

You know you are with the right person when he or she moves you into universal love. It doesn't just end at loving only one person. You have to expand your love to everything you come into contact with around that person. You know that's the case if he or she encourages you to share your love with the world. You would love to show him or her to the world. This person helps you expand your love energy. You can be yourself around him or her. He or she doesn't pretend to love you only when you are in a secret place with him or her.

Your true love would tell anyone that cares to know that he or she is in love with you. He or she will stand with you even in the most critical moments of your life. In a sense, yes, the person you get to marry “should complete you” and make you feel whole as a person, but you should already love who you are and feel blessed that the person you want to be with makes you feel even better.

You should be happy with who you are, what you do, and how you look. It will not only make it easier for you to attract people with your confidence, but it will make your life much better. So stop fantasizing about the person who can fill in all of the gaps in your unsatisfactory life.

Dear gentlemen, here are ways to know if she is the one:

- She is the first person you want to share your story with
- She’s excited to hear about your stories.
- Other attractive women seem less attractive to you since the day you encountered her.
- You always want to look better for her.
- You have your love languages that she understands.

Dear Ladies, here are ways to know if she is the one:

- He is the first person you want to share something with.
- He cares to know how you feel and listens to you.
- Other attractive men seem less attractive to you since you encountered him.

- You always want to look better for him at all times.
- He understands you and understands your love languages.

You should marry someone who entrusts you with their life. You need to know that trust is often earned, so let your partner earn your trust while you earn his or hers. Pretty lady, a man who wants to marry you will eventually open up to you when he notices that you are genuinely concerned about his welfare. We often term such a lady a "wife material".

He would have no choice but to start asking for your opinion on virtually everything. He would open up his inner thoughts, fears, and deep feelings to you. He would practically share his life with you. When all these signs pop up, then you know that he's gradually getting ready for marriage. Just give him that motherly love and care without judging him.

Even the toughest men often get emotionally soft when they have found the woman with whom they want to spend their lives. They are not scared to let you know how they feel. At such times, they are not ashamed to tell you how much you mean to them. They are always willing to tell you how special you are to them.

My handsome friend, you can find it very easy to penetrate

her heart; just show her how much you care and you are good to go!

My Poetic Advice to Single Ladies

Marry someone who is mature in mind, Not mature in body but childish in mind; Such can only build you a battleground.

Marry someone who is very sure of what they want, Not a confused being who likes to marry a slim lady But loves to hang out with all the chubby ladies.

Marry someone who accepts your physical appearance, Not someone who says she loves your slim and tall body But loves to flirt around town with huge and stout men.

Marry someone who treats you like a king or queen, Not someone who treats you like trash, who concludes That your opinion or feeling is in no way important.

Marry someone who will always believe in you, Not someone who thinks that the good of women Only ends in the "other" room at the very best.

Marry someone who respects the man in you, Not someone who only worships the money in you And ditches you when the going gets tough.

Marry someone who loves Christ with their life, And is willing to occupy His Priestly position In their life and marriage till He returns from above.

Not someone who will give up on Christ Because of the challenges of life that don't last. Not someone that strangles your faith in Christ!

CHAPTER THREE

SUCCESS IN MARRIAGE IS A CHOICE

While I was single, I had a severe fear of failed marriages, so I vowed within me that, with God's help, I would never fall victim to it. This singular ideology made me extremely careful about my choice of partner.

The first step I took in actualizing it was to build myself around people with positive vibes about marriage. To a large extent, one is affected by the associations to which one belongs and the people that one listens to.

I changed my circle immediately; I started listening to tapes, attending conferences, and reading many books on marriage. Then my mindset concerning marriage evolved in a positive way as I positioned myself to accept and build my marriage up to what I wanted it to be and how I wanted it to look.

Your success in marriage begins from your relationship stage. You don't beg a man or woman to love you; instead, you're to look out for someone who loves because you deserve it. Nobody should make you feel that they are doing you some favor by claiming to be in love with you.

You must not be loved by everyone; therefore, feel free to move away anytime or anywhere you perceive that you're treated as the last option. This is because if you continue to endure this situation during courtship, then you should be ready to continually dance to the tune when you eventually marry your partner.

A successful marriage starts from a successful relationship that one could build, keep, and nurture. There is an adage that as you make your bed, so you must lie on it. Thus, it is the kind of relationship that one could keep during courtship that would continue to play out even in marriage.

It's so pathetic to see some people during courtship allow certain attitudes from their partners, especially those that do not go down well with them. It is even more worrisome to note that many people who find themselves in this category often think that they would change everything in marriage. If I may ask, are you the Holy Spirit that changes a person?

It will be of utmost interest for these set of people to birth a change in their mind-sets and start making their wishes known to their partners earlier in courtship before the talk of marriage even crops up.

In building a successful relationship, you need to be put the key points below into consideration:

1. Choose wisely

When we choose to date people who are not fit for us, trying to use success strategies will have minimal impact.

For example, if I am with someone who doesn’t respect me or value our relationship, then improving my communication or intimacy skills will not make the person change a bit. To have a healthy relationship, we need to work to heal our issues so that we may begin to choose partners more wisely. Instead of choosing someone who is dysfunctional and then working and praying to change them, we need to become more practical and prayerful about the decisions we make before entering a relationship. In choosing wisely, you should acknowledge that you have a fault and so does the person you are dating. It will be in the interest of both of you to change your ill attitudes and pray over your relationship. You should realize that marriage is not simply one act but the beginning of a lifelong commitment. In every relationship, persistence and perseverance are key attitudes to continue staying stronger and better.

In choosing a partner, one should have a better understanding and good motives as regards the choice of partner he would like.

You should be willing to follow the lead of the Holy Spirit with the under listed guidelines:

- Begin by quieting your spirit and listening. God doesn't always come in dramatic ways like Moses encountered

Him on Mountain Sinai or Paul on the road to Damascus. Be willing to listen for the "gentle whisper" that Elijah heard (1Kings 19: 11-13).

- Open up your life totally to Jesus and seek the truth about yourself. Think about the things that you do that fall short of Christ-likeness and ask for forgiveness. Move to eliminate those behaviors.
- Ask the Holy Spirit to beam His convincing light on your right spouse. He will show you signs that will convince you that you are either with the right or wrong person. It could be through dreams, a conviction in the spirit through His voice of leading. When the revelation is not clear enough, it will be in your best interest to seek a spiritual guide from your clergy or guardian.

2. Marriage: put your heart into it

Marriage requires commitment, but some people don't commit that responsibility to heart. They fool themselves into thinking that it's like getting a new roommate, pooling their finances together, or an excuse to have an extravagant party. The truth is that marriage joins two people "for better or worse; for richer or poorer; in sickness and in health; to love and to cherish till death…." While those words sound wonderful, your actions determine the fate of your marriage.

People who put their heart into their marriage reap one of the greatest treasures in life. You'll have a soul mate to share your hopes and your fears; your laughter and your tears; your joy and your sorrow. The fact is that the love of your life will make your highs higher and your lows much easier to bear.

As Audrey Hepburn once said, "The best thing to hold onto in life is each other." Marriage is just the mathematical infinity; it offers no limit to your happiness. Anyone who desires success in marriage should have selfless interests and be willing to make sacrifices – loads of them.

Ensure that you share time with your spouse, family, and loved ones. Make out time for family time; spend holidays together. You shouldn't expect everything you say to be done; after all, no one is right all the time. You increase effective communication when you share ideas with your spouse and follow the one most suitable to put the family in a better condition.

You must be willing to celebrate each other's wins, no matter how little they might seem. Learn to admire, appreciate, and commend your spouse always; it strengthens the bond between you both. You must be willing to share the bed with your spouse, even when there is a misunderstanding.

I have seen a lot of people who after marriage prefer lying alone in a separate room and only meet their spouse for their conjugal right when need be. This attitude is wrong because even the Bible clearly states that a man shall leave his father and mother and cling unto a woman. The word cling means “to stick” as one, and you aren’t obeying the scriptures if you only meet your spouse in bed occasionally or even on-demand.

3. Be open to feedback

None of us is perfect and it is important for us to all realize there are ways by which we can improve. For your current relationship to succeed, you may need to learn some things that are different from the relationships you saw modeled for you when you were growing up and perhaps even strategies that are different from your previous relationships. Each person is different, so the things that worked with one person may not always work with every person. Communication is important so you can understand each other’s expectations, hopes, fears, and dreams.

No matter how you may be feeling, you should never neglect the communication key in your marriage: share your best moments with your spouse, be open and lend your voice when necessary.

Better communication between you and your partner leads

to more trust in each other, and better trust leads to more confidence. Effective communication techniques help to make you and your partner feel secure. Without that, it will be difficult for any relationship to thrive.

4. Keep it fresh

We mustn't take each other for granted. When we are initially dating, we often put our best foot forward, and then over time, we may see our efforts dwindling. We must let our partners know they are loved, desired, and appreciated. Look for creative ways to communicate your feelings to your partner. The love languages include expressing your feelings verbally, physically, with time, with gifts, and/or by actions that provide help for your partner. Think about which area your strength lies in and which area you can improve on. Always try to keep your relationship fresh.

5. Listen

In the event of any misunderstanding, many people often end up either talking back at each other or not speaking to each other. To keep the relationship going and growing, both people need to be heard. Instead of becoming defensive, try to listen to your partner's concerns. Even if you don't agree with everything, try to hear the inner issue or feelings that are motivating the statement of your partner.

After you have heard everything, let your partner know that you were listening to him or her by doing what you can to take into account his or her feedback. If people perceive that they are being ignored, they will simply shut down and stop sharing their issues. Successful couples listen to each other. Successful couples enjoy the different gifts that each one brings to the table. Both of you cannot be identical. Instead of trying to create a clone of yourself in your partner, learn to appreciate your partner for whom he or she is. This strategy can greatly reduce stress and tension between you and your partner and will allow you to truly enjoy your different personalities, styles, and preferences.

For your relationship to thrive, you have to invest your time, emotion, and effort. Success in a relationship or marriage is possible especially when both parties are willing to work for it and build it.

THINGS TO ENSURE AS YOU ESTABLISH A RELATIONSHIP

1. Ensure that you are attracted to each other

This is the very first part of a relationship. Before a relationship can be established between two parties, there must be something that attracts one to the other. Let us consider some of the vital characteristics that show that someone is attracted to you or vice versa.

When you're attracted to someone, it just means that your subconscious is attracted to their subconscious, subconsciously. So what we think of as fate is just two neuroses knowing that they are a perfect match in establishing a successful relationship.

First, there must be something that attracted you to the fellow, maybe his manner of speech. The Law of attraction is the first point. This is a crucial point in establishing a solid relationship. Both parties are meant to be attracted to each other. Human beings are wired to want intimate relationships; to love and be loved. Whether you're in an established long-term relationship or the first wonderful months of new love, doing some routine relationship maintenance is just a good idea. While every relationship is unique, there are a few tried and tested practices that can often help in giving just about any relationship a quick boost.

One of the greatest of such is ensuring that both parties are attracted to each other uniquely. Hopefully, this discussion can be a starting point from which you can be inspired and which you can use as a springboard to try some similar techniques that work for you and your partner specifically. After all, the secret to a happy relationship is often nothing more than just a little bit of effort.

2. Make sure to communicate

Communication is one of the top relationship goals to keep your bond stronger by the day. Everything from a simple text that says "hi" down to big conversations lets your partner know that they are in front of mind and you value their opinion (s). Making sure to talk to your partner about feelings – and making room for them to talk about theirs – is integral to a healthy relationship and strong emotional bond.

3. Understand each other

Not everyone speaks the same love language. Making the effort to understand the language your partner is speaking at each point in time is one of the best relationship goals to strengthen your bond. This could be through learning to read their body language, or it could be through simply talking more and being more open explaining your thoughts and feelings until your divergent points of view are fully understood by both of you.

If necessary, you may consider going to see a professional relationship counselor who can help you to better understand each other. When you understand not only what your partner is saying but how they're saying it, it allays their fear of being open and honest. The result is already known to us both.

4. Make time for yourself

While we all went to spend as much time with our partners as we can, it's important to make time for yourself as well. When you make time for your hobbies and spend some time with your friends, the time apart from your partner can make your bond stronger. You begin to want each other more when you miss each other a bit.

As Khalil Gibran wrote in The Prophet, "Let there be spaces in your togetherness and let the winds of Heaven dance between you." While sometimes we may think that time apart is always negative, it may be crucial in keeping the relationship alive.

Keep this relationship tip in mind to ensure that you find the right balance of "our time" and "my time". Find time for fun. Couples that still have fun and make each other laugh have some of the strongest bonds ever. Sometimes, just determine to let loose, be silly, try new things, revisit old things, and, most importantly, have fun. Your relationship will be the better for it. Even if it's just something as simple as mini-golfing or paint balling on date night, just let your hair down and have a little fun.

5. Grow together

As we move through life, we are all bound to change. Relationship goals will shift, but being in tune with your partner will keep you on the same page. Make time for weekly check-ins and talk about how each of you is feeling. This will go a long way towards making your bond that much stronger and get you closer to building the type of "couple goals" that people often talk about. It's as simple as it sounds: grow together.

6. Continue your courtship

Courtship is important before marriage, for it helps both of you to understand each other better and binds you both with stronger bonds. Even after marriage, continue trying to win each other over just the same way both of you were doing during courtship.

"Above all things, have fervent love for one another, for love will cover a multitude of sins "(1 Peter 4:8). "Be kindly affectionate to one another … in honor giving preference to one another" (Romans 12:10). Never go to bed angry with one another. "Do not let the sun go down on your wrath" (Ephesians 4:26). "Confess your trespasses to one another" (James 5:16), "Forgetting those things which are behind" (Philippians 3:13). "Be kind to one another, tenderhearted, forgiving one another, even as God in Christ forgave you" (Ephesians 4:32) "Her husband … praises her" (Proverbs 31:28). "She who is married cares … how she may please her husband" (1Corinthians 7:34).

To remain angry over hurts and grievances – big or little – can be dangerous. Unless addressed promptly, even little problems can become set in your mind as convictions and can adversely affect your outlook on life. This is why God teaches that you should let your anger cool before going to bed. Be big enough to forgive and say, "I'm sorry," even when you are not the one in the wrong. After all, no one is perfect, and you are both on the same team.

So be gracious enough to admit a mistake when you make one. Besides, making up is a very pleasant experience, with unusual powers to draw marriage partners closer together. God suggests it and it works!

7. Keep Christ in the center of your home

This is the greatest principle because it's the one that enables all the others. The vital ingredient of happiness in the home is not in diplomacy, strategy, or our effort to overcome problems, but rather in a union with Christ. "Unless the Lord builds the house, they labor in vain who build it" (Psalms 127:1).

Hearts that are filled with Christ's love will not be far apart for long. Jesus can wash away bitterness and disappointment and restore love and happiness. With Christ in the home, marriage has a greater chance of being successful.

"In all your ways acknowledge Him, and He shall direct your paths" (Proverbs 3:6). "And the peace of God, which surpasses all understanding, will guard your hearts and minds through Christ Jesus" (Philippians4:7).

8. Pray together

For a successful marriage, the couple should endeavor to live a life of prayer and fasting. The purpose of fasting is to influence God into acting on our behalf. Its purpose is to shut off the influence on our faith to be in tune with the Spirit (Mark 9:29). Fasting helps us to receive from God but does not push God into action. Abstaining from God does not impress Him.

Couples need to set aside time for effective and meaningful prayer. Make intercession for people who do not pray enough for their development, that is, children, cousins, friends, family, and enemies. In Ephesians 1:16, Paul prays for a "Spirit of wisdom and revelation".

As couples, say the prayer in Ephesians 1:16-23 for yourselves every day for one year, and God will open up your spirit and develop your understanding.

Prayer is very vital yet inevitable to every Christian. Through prayer, we make our request known to God. "Watch and pray, lest you enter into temptation. The spirit indeed is willing, but the flesh is weak" (Matthew 26:41).

"Pray for one another" (James 5:16). "If any of you lacks wisdom, let him ask of God, who gives to all liberally" (James 1:5).

You should also note that there is no particular time to pray, but praying without season is the perfect instruction Jesus gave to disciples. Some marital challenges are not ordinary, so it will be wise for couples to watch and pray for success in their marriage. Show me the couple that prays together and I will show you the marriage that will last forever.

9. The best time to pray is now.

Why wait for issues to arise before you could pray? Why wait until things go wrong before visiting your prayer altar? Why wait for the powers of your father's house to stop you before you could fight to the finish?

It's so appalling that many Christians fail to realize that there is spiritual empowerment we receive in our consistent prayer. A man stands as a father and a priest in his household. You're in charge, which means that your God has given you dominion to protect and control all happenings in your home. The woman stands as a help-meet to the husband. Both are working together in the actualization of the same purpose. Hence, they are to combine both forces in prayer.

WAYS TO BUILD A HAPPY AND LONG- LASTING MARRIAGE

Every individual is a free moral agent; thus, we decide what we want and apply practical efforts in achieving it. A happy and long-lasting marriage is achievable when the couples are ready to make it so. So if you desire to maintain a happy and long-lasting marriage, then the below tips are for you.

1. Love whom you married, not whom you wish you married

It is very hard for one to love someone they do not accept. This scenario has caused more harm than good in many marriages. Some humans are unsatisfied and ungrateful to the personality they married. They always see reasons to regret and wish they married someone else rather than their spouse. It will be of great advantage for one to accept the person that one has married and stop comparing them with anyone else.

2. Understand each other more than ever

Love will play its role excellently where there is understanding. Even the Bible reminds us that two cannot work together except they agree.

It is very important to note that it is the level of understanding that you share with your partner that will determine how much love you both will share because the simplest explanation of love is understanding.

No marriage succeeds without understanding. The willingness of one to accept the fact that the person they married is different from them they are will play a long role in building a successful relationship.

3. Communication is the key to the success of every marriage.

Effective communication plays a vital role in marriage as it stimulates love. You don't expect your spouse to guess what's on your mind without you voicing it out. Regardless of one's mood, it is right for you to share your mind with your partner. It will also relieve your mind.

4. Always speak well of your spouse both in his or her presence and absence.

It is the manner with which you respect and honor your spouse that will determine how other people will regard and treat him or her. You can't be speaking ill of your husband and expect others to respect and value him or her. So it is important that you both protect each other's image rather than washing your dirty linen in public.

5. You must be teachable to maintain a successful marriage.

Marriage consists of two genuine lovers who are willing to

accept each other's flaws and still maintain a peaceful atmosphere among each other. It is good to remind us that when you fall in love, you do not fall into a perfect person but into an imperfect person. This is also the reality for your partner.

However, you both will be perfected in love. No human is perfect in everything – you included. So if you are in for a successful relationship or marriage, then be ready to build it!

A successful marriage requires falling in love many times, always with the same person.

I remember when we were newly got married; I could say everything good about my spouse. If we ever had differences, we would try as much as possible to settle it privately at home and never in public. This has stimulated our love with the times and has always made people speak well of our marriage so much that we are now seen as pacesetters in our environment.

Sometimes, I see some persons lose interest in their spouse after few years of marriage, and that is when some of their marital problems set in. People have differences and couples are bound to disagree to agree, but it is how these differences are settled that shows the level of their maturity. To maintain a successful marriage, there is a need for one to push oneself to fall in love with the same person at all times. With this, it will be hard for you to think of someone as else more important than your spouse.

CHAPTER FOUR

THE POWER OF YOUR THOUGHT

For as a man thinketh in his heart, so is he (Proverbs 23:7).

Man is a trinity made up of spirit, soul, and body, or better put, man is a spirit with a soul living inside a body. The body is just a house where our souls, minds, or reasoning faculties dwell. Our spirits are the actual persons in which the soul or mind is housed in the heart. The heart is an organ in the chest that sends blood around the body.

However, the heart is the organ of all good and all evils.

The mind is the bedrock of evil. Evil thoughts emanate from the laboratory of the mind. There is no way an unclean person will be able to think about something good.

Who can bring a clean thing out of an unclean? Not one (Job 14:4)

This is a terrible condition for man. Man's actions and words are the products of the thought of the mind. The thought of the mind is powerful because it controls man both physically and spiritually. It controls the words of man.

For out of the abundance of the heart, the mouth speaketh (Mathew 12:34).

This is the reason many people talk anyhow because they

cannot control their thoughts. When one consistently thinks that one would never have a successful relationship with one's partner because of the fear of his or her failed relationships or because of people's opinions, it will continually be so because the person allowed his thought to guide him.

There is a negative saying that all men cheat. If one constantly believes this ill saying, then one is feeding the heart with negative thoughts. Before you realize it, you might start suspecting even your spouse to the extent of monitoring every of his or her little move. You might hardly believe anything he or she says, and this might even lead to a break-up. The reason is simple: trust is very crucial for a healthy relationship.

The heart is a major area of man's life that makes man helpless and opens the door wide for the wicked power to attack. The devil is always looking for a ladder to climb into somebody's life. That is why when he finds any opportunity through any negative-minded heart, he enters it to destroy the person.

Our thought is one of the weakest areas in our lives. We determine whatever we want to happen in our life through our thoughts. Many people think that happiness or success comes from around them. It doesn't. Happiness comes from the inside of us.

The way you think about yourself will determine the kind of life you want to live. If you always think positively about yourself, you will see things around you moving in a positive direction. But if you always think negatively about yourself, you will see things going in that direction.

A lady was dating a man for six years. She never disturbed the man to see her parents for any formal marital rites. They were together, thinking that they were enjoying themselves. The man told the lady that he was traveling home to see his sick mother, but he deceived her and went home to marry another lady. He paid the new lady's dowry, brought her to the city, and kept her somewhere else.

The news got to the first lady about what the man she loved had done. She couldn't bear the pain, so she committed suicide. Before she died, she dropped a note stating that she died because of what her would-be husband did to her.

Well, she wasted her life because she thought that her life was of no meaning to anyone. Her thought deceived her, making her see things as if there was no hope for her again. The devil knows how subtle thought can be; that is why he keeps using it to control man.

HOW TO CHANGE YOUR NEGATIVE THINKING PATTERN

If you are chronically negative, you can change your pattern of negative thinking. However, you have to want to make this change and no one can do it for you.

Here are some things you can do to be more positive:

- Avoid negative self-talk and stay positive

Because of the challenges of life, some people, including Christians, have allowed their problems to establish negative thoughts in them to the extent of harboring negative self-talk. Some begin to ask themselves, "Does God seem far away?" Some people have some significant emotional events that have happened in their life and they allow their past to shape their beliefs; they allow unresolved negative emotional events that happened in their past to come to the surface in their lives. So they can't get the positive ideas to release them from the unconscious blocks that have been preventing them from producing behaviors in alignment with their purpose in life.

People generate negative self-talk from the wiles of the trick of the devil. God says one thing and Satan says it is not so. Satan succeeds in deceiving them. That was the trick he used on Eve.

Do you know that before armed robbers start their

operations, something convinces them that everybody else in the world is a thief? And that nobody in this country is pure. Why? They have been deceived!

Some Wiles of the trick of the devil include miscarriage and suffering mentality.

- Miscarriage

Somebody believes God for a Child and gets pregnant. Suddenly, she sees blood. According to her, she has lost the child. That's the devil's lie! Is it blood you're pregnant with or a child? The blood you see is not a miscarriage; you're the one that gave it a name. That you're discharging blood while you're pregnant has nothing to do with the child in your womb.

I remember when I was pregnant with my first child. I first got a revelation about the pregnancy in the spirit when there wasn't any form of evidence in the physical. Few weeks after the revelation, I began to see blood. I wanted to believe it was a miscarriage or a normal monthly circle, but I bless my husband, the priest over my life.

He encouraged me and declared a convincing word that he was sure of what God had shown us – that I was pregnant. He further charged my Spirit that no matter the amount of blood coming out, that was meaningless. Before this charge, I had run several pregnancy tests in the hospital on different occasions and all medical results proved me negative to pregnancy.

I went into a state of dilemma, but I summoned the courage to stand on the words of the Lord concerning my pregnancy. I almost waited for six months before my spirit convinced me to repeat the same pregnancy test. Lo and behold, the test confirmed that I had been pregnant all the while for five months and few weeks! What a great God, the miracle-working Father!

The gift and calling of God are without repentance. Children are a blessing from the Lord. Whatever God has blessed people with, He does not withdraw. Did He not assure us in Exodus 23:26b that for those who serve Him, none shall miscarry or be barren in your land?

Don't let the devil specialize any problem for you. Whatever it is you're going through, it is not peculiar to you alone (1 Corinthians 10:13). Don't let the devil make life tense for you.

- Suffering Mentality

This is another evil device of the devil with which he deceives souls.

Jesus said in Mathew 11:29, "Take my yoke upon you, and learn of me; for I am meek and lowly in heart: and ye shall find unto your souls."

This is what the Master has said, yet some people believe that difficulties are the things that give meaning to Christianity. Suffering and sorrow to them are the only ways to categorize righteousness.

Ninety percent of preachers don't bother to read the scriptures. Though you see trouble on the way, the owner of the way says it is an easy road, that the journey to heaven is an easy one. Bless God for Jesus; we can walk in the truth, while we're here on earth!

So get rid of such mentality, for you are a king in God. Or can you name me just one king who lives in abject poverty?

2. Be vulnerable

Another way to be positive in thought is by being vulnerable. No mistake here: vulnerability is strength, not weakness, and opening up to someone who can help you will free you from all the feelings and emotions that have been preventing you from living in alignment with love and joy.

Anyone who is going through any form of negative self- talk should realize that they are worthy of love and everything that they dream of regardless of what happened in the past. You should start producing behaviors and taking actions in alignment with your new belief.

Oswald Chambers advises us:

Get into the habit of dealing with God about everything. Unless in the first waking moment of the day you learn to fling the door wide back and let God in, you will work on a wrong level all day; but swing the door wide open and pray to your Father in secret, and every public thing will be stamped with the presence of God. When God is all you have, then He is all you need.

Draw near to God, and He will draw near to you (James 4:8). The Bible also says that God is never more than a prayer or praises away. That's the good news!

Tommy Barnett reflected, "The deeper I dig, the deeper He digs." So to increase value, get to know God. Our prayer to God should be "I want to be in your will, not in your way."

Our heartfelt cry to God can be the same as Isaiah's: "Here I am, send me" (Isaiah 6:8).

Consider the word of W.H. Atken when he said, *"Lord take my lips and speak through them; take my mind and think through it; take my heart and set it on fire."* We must not only give what we have, but we must also give all of what we are to God.

3. Appreciate each other

When you're with someone all the time, it's easy to take them for granted, but according to MacGregor, you should verbally express your appreciation every day. Whether you’re calling positive attention to something thoughtful they've done, or letting them know something you like about them. “We all need to feel appreciated and reinforced for the things we are doing right,” says MacGregor, “If we don’t feel valued we may become resentful and grow apart.’’

For example, if your spouse makes you coffee in the morning, tell him or her that it started your day with a smile. Some people have allowed comparison to devour a big part of them. Instead of being happy with their spouse, they keep comparing their marriage and their spouse with anyone else. Hear me: comparison is a joy killer; it would never allow one to see the good part of their spouse.

I remember a brother who came complaining that his wife had been raining insults on him, stressing that he was not giving her the best life she deserved. This is the same woman for whom her husband opened a business, was providing virtually everything she at home, and had even promised to do more. That attitude arose only because of what the wife saw a lady on social media whose fiancé had engaged with a brand new modern car.

The second example is a woman whose husband gifted a car on her birthday. The woman started demanding that the husband buy her a particular car, that those riding it are still human just like her. They were just a young couple who were still struggling to meet their basic financial needs. They were just on their building stage, but even though her husband established a business for her, she wasn't satisfied. This brought serious quarrels for the couple but to the glory of God, they settled their differences after my relationship counsels.

RENEW YOUR MIND

And be renewed in the Spirit of your mind (Ephesians 4:23).

There is a saying that what you constantly say or believe is what comes your way.

Your mind is a magnet.

If you think of blessings, you attract blessings.

But if you think of problems, you attract problems.

Always cultivate good thoughts and always remain optimistic.

You need a fresh baptism of mind renewal. It's time to build a mental picture of a glorious life that transcends the limits of your emotional thoughts and your family background.

Always remind yourself that every evil word proceeds out of your thought.

For instance, a man who gets to the point of slapping his wife already had the plot planned out in his mind first.

Likewise, the couple who cheat on each other had already allowed their hearts to be littered with evil thoughts before the actual act of cheating on each other.

What do you do to your mind to make it resist the enemy's pollution? Your mind must be correctly tuned to God to know exactly what to do per time. You need to "spiritualize" your mind.

For to be carnally minded is death: but to be spiritually minded is life and peace (Romans 8:6).

Satan took over the minds of Peter and Judas. Thanks to God, Peter eventually overcame his temptation, but Judas ended up a victim. Satan took over the mind of Eve and she shifted her mind from God's commandment. According to Paul's writing to the Corinthian church, Eve was deceived; she wasn't overpowered (2 Corinthians 11:3; 2 Timothy 3:13).

Thou wilt keep him in perfect peace, whose mind is stayed on thee… (Isaiah 26:3).

Let God take charge of your mind and you will know perfect peace. If you give your mind over to the devil, he will steal your destiny. Be at alert!

When the devil comes to clog your mind with wild imaginations and thoughts, clear your mind up by praying in the Holy Ghost (Jude 20). That will ventilate your mind.

You might be telling yourself, "I want to enjoy life; I want to be in the will of God; I want to marry God's will but my mind seems to be an enemy of my soul and future." For things to work out well for you, your mind's world must be in good participation with that of your spirit.

You must constantly have a spiritual perspective on life. It doesn't matter if the entire universe is falling apart. Being swallowed up in problems just won't affect you as much if you stay spiritually-minded. Being spiritually- minded is life and peace. Never listen to what the devil is saying. If he tries to show you how many marriages have failed, show him the countless unions that have and are still succeeding. At all times, be mindful of what God is saying.

You must see things the way God sees them. You must not be overtaken by what is happening around you. Spiritually-minded people are people of exploit, as they must enjoy life and peace.

And be not conformed to this world: but be ye transformed by the renewing of your mind, that ye may prove what is that good and acceptable and perfect will of God (Romans 12:2).

It is never God's will for your marriage to fail, so why think in that direction? Even when the storm of life comes, speak peace to that storm and it will be calm. You will enjoy a heaven-on-earth marriage if you follow God's lead.

Let your mind be constantly flushed with God's Word. Let God's Word give you a new thought pattern; let it affect your mind positively.

You need a daily renewal of your mind, for it will help you to disregard the enemy and all his pranks. You will then find yourself looking at life with hope. People who never encounter any problem in their Christian encounters are those who have been designed to excel without much trouble. You could be among that number if only you are willing to keep a positive mind.

I once met a woman who had been married for many years without conceiving. She had tried many ways to conceive but they all proved abortive. After she encountered counseling sections and prayers with me, I prophetically declared to her to go and produce babies.

For some reason, I lost her contact. Then one day, I visited an office for a function. Little did I know that it was the same woman's office. I could no longer recall her face. She approached me and started identifying herself with me because obviously, I couldn't remember her due to some changes that had taken place. She kept trying to make me remember her, but I just couldn't. It was not until she mentioned that she was the woman for whom I prophesied prayed concerning the fruit of the womb. “Oh my!” went I. I was so shocked because she already had a baby with her as we spoke. Indeed, that strengthened my faith further on the fact that there is nothing God cannot do.

Don’t ever let the enemy tell you that your future has no meaning. You are invaluable to God. The whole world cannot compare with the value of your soul. So you are precious to God.

God is not behind your sufferings. He is standing there to lift you out of your suffering if you would let Him. He takes pride in your success. He wants to brag about you. So do not let the enemy fool you into believing that nothing else matters except getting to heaven. You are not only to get to heaven but you are to radiate his glory also upon the earth. And that is actually how you can get to heaven – by showing God to the world through your life.

I don’t pity someone who is a failure. All I do is tell them, “Stand up from where you are and find your way out. You don’t belong there!” Stop living a fake life. Get a correct perspective of life. Tell yourself that you will no longer be an object of pity. See yourself from now on as a blessing and source of happiness to others, and not dying as a beggar.”

Those who have polluted minds can never see a positive future for themselves in this life. Their consequently lose their destinies to circumstances of life. They walk on in hopelessness and frustration. Always remember that your mind belongs to God and keep it pure.

What you watch or listen to is like food to your soul; your mind begins to work within that perspective. For many people, instead of listening to stories of successful relationships and happy marriages, they keep searching for news about failed relationships and marriages. They keep at this to the extent that they fill their hearts with evil thoughts and believe that "there is no successful marriage".

This thought then leaves them in psychological bondage and turns affects their marriages negatively.

For some other people, because of what they hear about someone, they live with hatred for the said fellow, so much that no matter what the person does, they never value or appreciate that person.

Your thoughts shape your life (Proverbs 4:23). Think about good things only. Anytime you find yourself thinking about trash, tell your mind to come back home, even if it means yelling at yourself aloud in public.

When you hear people say such things as "marriage is a scam," the Bible tells us, "Beware!" God says His plan for you is to have positive welfare and a bright future. However, what God ends up doing with you is limited to what expectations you have.

If you have a mediocre expectation, that's where you'll end up. But if you have a superior expectation, that's exactly where you'll reach.

"For as he thinketh in his heart, so is he" (Proverb 23:7).

The right expectations don't beget anxiety; rather, they make you walk in peace and serenity.

Overall, keep in mind Dr. Gottman's 5:1 ratio relationship principle: "For every negative, create five positives." No relationship or marriage is perfect. There can be challenges at times, but having fun, being open to communication, and enjoying each other's company are some of the keys to a healthy and happy relationship or marriage.

HAVE ENOUGH…

Have peace enough to press on.

Have hope enough to keep your heart looking forward.

Have strength enough to battle obstacles and overcome them.

Have commitment enough to not give up too soon. Have fun enough to enjoy every aspect of life.

Have patience enough to let faith complete its work in you.

Have love enough to give to those who deserve it the least

but need it the most.

Have focus enough to say "no" to many good ideas.

Have forgiveness enough to never end the day hating someone.

Have honesty enough to never have to remember what you said.

Have character enough to do in the light what you would do in the dark.

Have gratitude enough to say "thank you" for the things that matter less.

Have purpose enough to know why and not just how.

Have perseverance enough to run the entire race that is set out before you.

Have responsibility enough to be the most dependable person you know.

Have kindness enough to share what you have and who you are with others.

Have mercy enough to forgive and forget.

Have devotion enough to do the right things daily.

Have courage enough to face and fight any opposition to what you know is right.

Have expectancy enough to be on the lookout for opportunities every day.

Have obedience enough to do what is right without

thinking twice.

Have direction enough to know when and where to go.

Have knowledge enough to continually educate your mind.

Have credibility enough to cause others to want to work together with you.

Have generosity enough to give before being asked.

Have compassion enough to be moved by the needs of others.

Have loyalty enough to be committed to others. Have joy enough to transmit happiness to others.

Have courage enough to confront the challenges that might come your way.

Have discipline enough to keep positive thoughts, no matter what happens!

CHAPTER FIVE

THINGS TO CONSIDER BEFORE SAYING I DO

Desire Is Arbitrary; Intention Is Commitment

If you do not commit to turning your desires into reality by being intentional, you will continue to daydream about things that will never happen. The dating and engagement periods of your relationship are a beautiful time for both of you. Romance is blossoming, you're building dreams together, and anything seems possible.

When we're dating, we often overlook some areas of our lives that we need to consider before walking down the aisle. In the haze of falling in love and promised happily- ever-after, there are the things you should consider.

Every lady loves to see a man with all his manly ego and masculinity, who leaves everything aside for a moment, goes down on one knee before his lady, brings out a diamond-crusted ring, and utters those four sweet, romantic words – will you marry me? It is an adorable sight, right? Every lady loves this moment; it is magical. The romance in it is unexplainable; it's like a dream come true.

However, it doesn't end there. The aim shouldn't be to hurriedly say yes to a man; it should be to say yes to the right man. Marriage is one long-distance trip, and you know that there are so many things to ensure before venturing on this distant trip.

IMPORTANT THINGS EVERY LADY SHOULD CONSIDER BEFORE SAYING 'YES'

1. Is he true to you?

You have to be sure that the man to whom you are about to say yes is honest with you, with his words, and with his actions. If he's deceitful to you in the course of the relationship, then you shouldn't expect anything better when you bear his name.

Your man has to be honest with you; he has to be true to you. Lying shouldn't be an option, nor should unfaithfulness. Deceit shouldn't even be in the picture for him. Surprisingly, some ladies say yes to men that they don't even know much. You have to know your man deep down.

2. Financial stability

I'm one of those who kick against ladies that are only there for the money but it also doesn't mean that you should sign your death certificate and enter a marriage headed for poverty.

Your man should be able to foot the basic bills at least. Even if he cannot afford most things at that point, you have to be sure that he has prospects and plans in that regard. Do not get married to a man that has no money but is without a feasible plan to make money. Trust me; poverty in marriage is almost like a death sentence.

3. His temperament

This is one thing many ladies fail to analyze before saying yes to a man. A man's temperament is crucial. If, for instance, he can't control his anger, then one person would suffer severely from it – and that is you.

Don't get married to a man that would turn you into his punching bag. It isn't worth the hassle. If he can't control his temper, then you are at risk of coming into harm's way. Domestic violence is in the waiting for you, and it's no fun.

4. His love for you

Does he love you genuinely? Can he go the extra mile for your sake? Is he honest about his feelings for you? Does he think you are special? Would his love stand the test of time or is it just ordinary? These questions are important questions you should be sure of before that ring slips into your finger.

5. Your feelings for him

The first four tips centered mainly on the man, but it doesn't just end there. It's not all about the man. Many ladies marry even when they are so unsure of the feelings they have for their man. You have to be sure that you love that man for real. There is no negotiating this; if you don't love him, there should be no need to tie the knot with him.

Marriage is no small affair; a time would come when the chips would be so down, and the only thing that would keep you going is your love for him. So if the affection isn't real, then the marriage won’t last.

6. How ready are you?

Marriage is different from a dating relationship. You might be ready for a relationship but not ready for marriage. To have a successful marriage, you should be willing to make a lot of sacrifices. If you aren't ready for those sacrifices, then you are not fit for marriage.

7. Do you love someone else?

You have to sort yourself out before you say yes to a man. The dilemma of being married and still in love with someone else is one that you should avoid. If he isn’t the only one your heart is set out for, then you shouldn’t hurriedly say yes; else, you would successfully start a journey where the endpoint would be a total fatality.

8. Can you tolerate him?

You and I know that no one is perfect. If you are expecting to marry a perfect man or woman, then it’s about time you woke up to the realities of life. Make sure that the person is someone that you can tolerate, someone for whom you are willing to make sacrifices.

You cannot like everything about your partner, but you must

be more than willing to accept him or her that way.

9. Make sure you are not lured by the wrong motives

I am not out to play the role of judge and jury, but you have to satisfy your conscience for the reasons you have chosen to say yes to your man. If your reasons aren't good enough, then you should know that he isn't your man. But just like the fifth tip pointed out above, if your feelings are genuine, then you should give it a go.

Don't get lured into marriage for the wrong reasons; they won't last. You would probably get tired of them at a point. Marriage is supposed to be a lifetime event, so if you get married for the wrong reasons, then at some point it would eventually tell on you.

10. Weigh your collective goals

Before you leap the lifelong covenant of marriage, it's important to consider the goals and dreams that both of you are nurturing. Will you be able to support one another's passions and pursuits? How will your marriage affect your goals and vice versa?

FIVE THINGS A MAN SHOULD CONSIDER BEFORE SAYING 'I DO'

Before a man speaks the official nuptial words, there's no doubt that his mind would be thinking ahead to the future, picturing himself as an actual husband, and her as a lawful wife. If he doesn't already have any little kid, he'd be picturing himself as a dad. Sounds pretty grown-up, right? However, it doesn't just happen from the moon. A man must have thought through some things before being convinced to proceed with the official words. Here below are five of those key issues that a man must consider before going ahead to tie the knot.

1. Family

Your family of origin has tremendous influence over your past, present, and future. Depending on the circumstances, the different families you come from could have a tremendous impact on your relationship.

There's a popular African saying that when you get married, "you marry the family" as well. That's true to a large extent. Take a close look at the home that your intended wife comes from. Is it toxic and unhealthy? If you don't trace it on time, it's possible that those damaging patterns can make their way into your marriage and the family you plan to build together.

A difficult past or an abusive family of origin isn't the death sentence for your relationship, but it is something you should carefully consider. If this is the scenario you find yourself facing, you two may seek counseling together. It could help both of you to prevent bad family patterns from sneaking into your home in the future. A stitch in time, they say, saves nine. Do your due diligence before uttering those official words.

2. Belief

Spirituality is one of the biggest hot-button issues in relationships. It is deep, personal, and can be a very volatile subject. This is all the more reason to talk it out early enough.

Holding different belief systems doesn't mean that your marriage cannot work, but you'll have some very challenging waters to navigate as a couple, especially between your different families.

A host of pressures will come your way, which is why you should have figured things out before getting to the aisle.

3. Mindset

Is the glass half empty to her, or is it half full? How does she approach the world? Is it with optimism, pessimism, or realism? Your mindset is the lens through which you view the world and if your different mindsets clash with the other, it might be difficult to face life's ups and downs together.

If you view the world through a positive, optimistic lens and your partner views it from a negative, pessimistic angle (and vice versa), then it would be hard to team up during all the battles that you'll face in life. These battles are inevitable.

Listen to her and observe her; you may even ask her questions to grasp her mindset.

4. Compatibility

How well do you get along? What's your level of rapport with each other? Being compatible with each other's personalities and mannerisms is a very important factor to consider when you're thinking about getting married.

Opposites can indeed attract opposites and remain compatible. But sometimes, our differences can throw us a curve ball, and it's helpful to know what those differences are and how to navigate them.

You might be very attracted to each other right now, but if you don't get along well, the attraction could fade out with time.

Compatibility is one key measure that would eventually lead to a successful marriage. The issue of compatibility shouldn't be taken for granted at all, for any reason whatsoever. When you and your partner are compatible, your marriage is blissful and a joy to watch.

On the other hand, when compatibility is lacking in your marriage, it transforms into a cat-and-rat affair.

5. Priority

What's most important to each of you? You'll find that the everyday priority you both hold will tell you a lot about each other. Verbalizing priority isn't enough; you must watch each other's actions to discern for yourself what things take precedence in your lives.

You should determine whether your priorities align, or whether they might cause conflict in a marriage situation. It's not easy to anticipate challenges you might face in the future when you're in love or when you are dating, but conflicting priorities in a marriage will quickly send you down a path you would not love to follow.

You might be wondering if you should think over all these things within a split second before saying yes or I do (as the case may be). That shouldn't be the case; all these factors should be evaluated while the relationship is still ongoing.

As a lady, you don't have to wait till he brings out a ring and goes down on one knee before you browse through the ideas. Never so! As a man, you have to do your assignment early before it is too late to say never.

With a proper evaluation of the above factors, you would know whether you're ready and whether he or she is ready, too.

Rushing into marriage with him might be too risky as

divorce might loom about that marriage not too long after. If you aren't careful, your marriage with her might as well be a capsizing boat from the word go.

Therefore, you both must do your due diligence; know your spouse (KYS).

CHAPTER SIX

BEWARE OF DEPRESSION

Depression

The dictionary meaning of depression shows that it is a feeling of utter hopelessness, despondence, self-disgust, and loss of perspective. It is a mood swing into which a man is cast.

Who is the author? Satan, the enemy! Depression chokes the brain; it robs the mind (Luke 8:14). It blinds the mind (2 Corinthians 4:4). It is a very destructive weapon of the enemy which we must fight. It is a destroyer that makes victims of men.

Depression enters into the mind to cut it off from the light of the glorious gospel. It chokes the Word and makes the mind unproductive.

When you are depressed, your access to God's presence is blocked (Psalm 100:1-5). Depression disconnects you from the Father. It destroys your harvest. If the devil can get you depressed any day, he has spoilt your day.

Depression brings a man under a curse (Deuteronomy 28:47-48). It is the worst enemy of your destiny.

Depression retards your flight to your high places, has your high places and has your joy cut off (Habakkuk 3:17- 19).

Satan brings worries and anxieties to keep you down. Consequently, the Word of God becomes meaningless and unimportant to you.

Move away from any depressed person; they can depress your life. Depression can destroy your health, which Satan wants to destroy.

The moment you give in to depression, the things that should be working start failing. Whereas sins are unforgivable, we should treat depression because it is a sin against oneself, not against God. So deal with it!

Satan may present to you many reasons why you should be in depression, but your winning power lies on many reasons through God's Word.

WHY YOU SHOULD NOT BE DEPRESSED

Even if it seems your relationship is not working out, your marriage is on the verge of breaking, and many more, they are not good reasons why you should be depressed. Instead, find the antidotes to depression in the ideas below and apply them where necessary.

- Self-care to Depression

One can help oneself walk out of depression by taking enough sleep, eating a nutritious diet, and not misusing any form of alcohol or drugs to cope. These can also help you feel better faster.

Another form of self-care to consider is exercise. Research shows that exercising three times a week between 20 to 40 minutes can help reduce depression symptoms. It is not only for the moment but also long term. So walking, running, or joining a fitness class may help.

Understandably, many people with depression struggle with self-care during episodes. When this occurs, other treatment options may be required until the depression is at a level where self-care feels more manageable.

In general, depression rubs one's internal peace of mind, and happiness will be far-fetched. People get depressed when certain occurrences take place in their lives – when they lose their loved ones, get stressed up in their workplaces, experience mental retardation and emotional stress due to failed relationships, find it difficult to get a wife or a husband, fall into wrong marriages, have late marriages, live through fruitless marriages, live with unsupportive spouses, live with quarrelsome spouses, and many more.

All these might be some of the reasons why many are depressed. However, the good news is that there is only one unique antidote for depression that will make you live a happy life.

This truth is not far-fetched, for it is written in God's Word, which is the most trusted comfort in our times of sorrow or depression. Find solace in His Word.

- Rejoice Evermore!

Joy is the secret of our superiority over Satan. Depression makes victims of men, but joy makes champions of men.

Rejoice in the Lord always; and again, I say, rejoice (Philippians 4:4).

Joy is a pacesetter in our Christian race. The more of it you have, the more victories you enjoy over Satan. The only medicine for depression is joy. It is the only way to ventilate your spirit. If you're merry, sing. (James 5:13).

When you're depressed, you have no contact with God's presence. A "praiseful" life is what is required to carry God's presence with you anytime, anywhere. Without joy, you have no access to revelations (Isaiah 12:3). Without revelation, there's no faith, and without faith, there is no victory (1 John 5:4). Joy always makes your day!

Serve the Lord with joyfulness and gladness of heart, and Satan will have no access to you. Satan is out to move you against God. Keep him off with joy – singing and making melody in your heart unto the Lord (Ephesians 5:19).

Organize your soul for joy and happiness. Program your heart for it. Fill your house with music. Live in constant gratitude and thankfulness to God. To take God for granted is to be grounded. Let your heart dwell in a ceaseless flow of thanksgiving and appreciation unto God. There is nothing in this world that should be allowed to destroy your eternity. People who are cheaply moved never live to move their mountains.

The level of joy at which you operate determines the level of exploits you enjoy. It makes you and God a formidable or an invincible team. It establishes your triumph over Satan during any conflict of life.

Heaviness is a spirit (Isaiah 61:3). It is one of the key strategies of Satan to strip God's people naked. Satan calculated heaviness for God's people because he knows that no one can stop the fiery act of God whenever man is giving God quality praise. So fight heaviness with joy.

Every time you can't find joy, the thief is at work. The devil comes to steal your joy so that he can make a victim of you. But a ceaseless flow of joy will cause your spiritual life to blossom. Engage in this heavenly sense to be free from depression.

- Past Times

There is no future in the past. As Mike Murdock would say, "Stop looking at where you have been and start looking at where you can be." The past will always be the way it has been, so stop trying to change it. Rosy thoughts about the future can't exist when your mind is full of the blues about the past.

The more you look back, the less you will get ahead. Thomas Jefferson was right when he said, "I like the dreams of the future better than the history of the past." In the same vein, I agree with Laura Palmer's advice: "Don't waste today regretting yesterday instead of making a memory for tomorrow."

As David McNally puts it, "You cannot change your past, but you can change your tomorrow by your actions today." It's also true what Satchel Paige said, "Don't look back. Something might be gaining on you." How about the words of wisdom in the book of Proverbs? "The wise man looks ahead. The fool attempts to fool himself and won't face the facts" (Proverbs 14:8).

The first rule for happiness is: avoid lengthy thinking about the past. Nothing is as far away as one hour ago. "Living in the past is a dull and lonely business; looking back strains the neck muscles, causing you to bump into people not going your way" (Edna Ferber).

Bear these wise words of advice and encouragement in mind at all times to keep a positive mindset and say no to depression.

- The More You Look Backward, the Less You'll See Forward

Yesterday ended last night. So today, it is more valuable to look ahead and prepare than to look back and regret. Don't let regrets replace your dreams. "A man is not old until regrets take the place of dreams" (John Barrymore). Regret looks back; worry looks around; while vision looks up.

We can understand life backward, but we must live it forward. Your past relationship is the start of your new relationship. If history were all that mattered, librarians would be the only successful people in the world. You should only view the past with gratitude for the good things therein. Therefore, you should only look backward with gratitude but look forward with confidence.

Consider what Vivian Laramore said, "I've shut the door on yesterday and have thrown the key away – tomorrow holds no fears for me since I've found today."

You must use the past as a launching pad, not a lawn chair. Dreams of the future are more valuable than the history of the past.

At best, experience is yesterday's answer to today's problem. Your past is not your best potential. Never build your future around your past. The past is over. To succeed, you must be willing to shed part of your previous life.

"Keep your eye on the road, and use your rear-view mirror only to avoid trouble" (Daniel Meacham). Stop taking your steps backward. It is more valuable to look where you're going than to see where you've been. Don't see your future only from the perspective of yesterday. It's too easy to limit everything and hinder the dream within you.

You can never plan the future by just looking at the past. Those to whom yesterday still looks big aren't doing much today. *"The past should be a springboard, not a hammock,"* says Edmund Burke.

Your future contains more happiness than any past you can remember. Don't look at your past to determine your future. You can't walk backward into the future. You can find true misery by being a yesterday person trying to get along with a tomorrow world. Don't let your past mistakes become memorials. They should be cremated, not embalmed.

Some people stay so far in the past that the future is gone before they get there. The future frightens only those who prefer living in the past. No one has ever backed into prosperity. You can't have a better tomorrow if you are thinking about yesterday today.

Yesterday has passed forever and is beyond our control. What lies behind us is insignificant compared to what lies ahead. Those who predominantly talk about the past are going backward. Those who discuss the future are growing.

Choose where you belong. But I would be happy for you if you choose to look forward and let go. It will help you wave depression one final bye.

LET IT GO

Some people walk away from you;

When people walk away from you, let them go.

Don't talk another person into staying with you; let them go.

Don't talk another person into caring about you; let them go.

Don't talk another person into coming to you; let them go.

Don't talk another person into attaching to you; let them go.

When people walk away from you, let them walk;

Your destiny is never tied to anybody that left; let them leave.

People leave you because they are not joined to you; let them leave.

And if they are not jointed to you, why should you bother? Let them leave.

Know when people's part in your story is over and let them go.

So do not keep trying to raise the dead; let them go. Stop begging people to stay, let them go.

Once you get to know when it's dead, let it go.

If you are holding on to something that doesn't belong to you, let it go;

It is not meant for your life, so you need to let it go.

If you are holding on to the past that hurts and pains, let it go.

If someone has annoyed you, let it go.

If you are holding unto evil and revenge, let it go.

If you are involved in a wrong relationship, let it go.

If you are holding on to a job that no longer meets your needs or talent, let it go.

If you are weighed down by addiction, let it go. If you have a bad attitude, let it go.

If you keep judging others to make yourself feel better, let it go.

If you are struggling with healing a broken relationship, let it go.

If you are trying to help someone who is not even trying to get help, let it go.

If you are feeling depressed and stressed, let it go.

Let the past be in the past, forget old things, and let it go!

The bottom line is that there is no point holding on to a particular thing when it is not giving you your desired output. Instead of thinking about it until it breaks you down, let it go. Life will always continue no matter what happens if you allow the devil he will take control of your life through your thought.

The Bible admonishes us that we should have the mind of Christ. Let this mind be in you as it was also in Christ Jesus (Phil. 2:5). When you have the mind of Christ Jesus, you will be able to control your thoughts and words; the devil will not control your thoughts and words. The devil will not control you anymore and will not keep you in any form of bondage.

The mind of Christ will always show love and would be ready at all times to let go of anything that might want to give the devil a chance. You need this mind of Christ Jesus to let go and conquer depression.

CHAPTER SEVEN

HOW I MET AND GOT MARRIED TO MY HUSBAND

After my secondary education, I went further to gain computer skills while awaiting admission to study my dream course. During my first few weeks in the institution, I noticed a handsome man, and I loved every aspect of his appearance. This ranged from his charming eyes to his pointed nose. Even his masculine physique was top-notch.

In my heart, I just muttered, “Men, this guy is cute.” But I did not commit his handsome appearance to heart because I never wanted an “every woman’s dream” as my man. I just concluded him to be a womanizer because of how attractive he was. That thought made me overlook him without showing any level of interest.

One day, while I was chatting with a friend, he beckoned me to call my friend. That was the very first day he noticed me. It happened that while I was there to study computer software packages, he was into programming and repairs.

Fast forward to the day I had an oral presentation at the institute; I observed him as he constantly stared at me in awe of my presentation. The expression on His face left me with the conviction that he loved what he saw.

Just immediately after the training, he congratulated me and appreciated my efforts. I felt so fulfilled and emotional about that meeting.

Few days after the presentation, he opened up his intention to marry me. I was just surprised and happy at the same time. It was a thing of joy that we had the same thought about each other, though I never expected him to propose that soon.

I never gave him an immediate answer concerning his request but urged him to give me a little time to pray over it and receive direction from God.

Meanwhile, we became friends and things were going well with us but I was unserious with the prayer. It was not until he pressurized me, saying that he had had his revelation and was convinced that I am to be his wife.

My first question to him was, "Your financial status isn't encouraging; is this how you are going to marry me?" He felt a bit embarrassed but maintained his composure and smiled at me.

"You need to properly establish yourself financially before talking about marriage with me," I stressed further. I encouraged him to leave his father's house and fend for himself. I made him realize that his ability to be independent is a great score for him while talking about marriage, for no parents would entrust their daughter to a stranger who is still dependent. Of course, he obliged my advice and began to make feasible plans.

Just after a short while, he announced to me that he would be traveling to a particular state. He sincerely confessed that I had opened his eyes to some hidden challenges of his life, which had indirectly motivated him to take deliberate actions.

Even though he wasn't certain about his accommodation and any job opportunity at his destination, he insisted on traveling. He needed independence.

All the while that he was away, we never ceased to communicate with and encourage each other.

Most Christian singles talk about how they are waiting on God to give them their future spouse pretty often. We all want love and we want God to give us the right person to marry. We want God to bless us and sometimes we get angry when He hasn't. I want to ask you two big questions that you should take a second to think about: "What if God never gives you a spouse? Would you still love him in any case?"

Hopefully, your answer is yes. God wants us to put Him first, not a spouse. I'll tell you from experience; it is possible to be happy with God and no spouse. I prayed to God many times to bless me with the bone of my bone because I believed that marrying the right spouse would help me live a fulfilled life. I put God first because I knew that a spouse would never make me happy without Him being in the center of my life. I finally figured that out after many failed relationships. This is not to say I didn't want a spouse anymore, but if God never gives me one, that's fine since it's His will. I always believe that He has big plans for me than I am focused on right now.

Being single is a good thing. Check out 1 Corinthians 7:8; Paul says, "To the unmarried and the widows, I say that it is good for them to remain single as I am." It gives us time to get closer to God, which is the number one reason we are on earth. You can then add helping others get to know Him as the next key reason.

Only God can truly make us happy. Ever seen a miserable married couple? Yea, they are everywhere. Having a spouse is not the solution to your problems. Married Christians struggle, too. We struggle our entire lives, no matter what our relationship status is.

It is better to embrace it than try to fight it and be angry about it because once we do, our perspectives change. It's either we cast our cares on God or let them pile up onto our shoulders.

How many times have you fallen already? God also wants you to work on yourself. Ask yourself this: "Am I ready for a spouse?" And be honest about this question because if you are single, that means you are not ready. This is not to insinuate that there is anything wrong with us but that we have other things we need to focus on first. We have to do what God asks or we will keep waiting and waiting until we are old and wiry. Hopefully, you're saved. That is step one. Look at Acts 2:38 if you are not sure.

Let me take you through the rest of my marriage story. One night, as we were discussing over the phone, my man reminded me that I had not given him a reply regarding his proposal to me. That same night, I became serious about obtaining answers from God. I sought His face as never before.

God spoke in the end, approving him as my would-be husband. Even though God revealed him to be His will for me regarding my marriage, it felt as if I wasn't ready. I needed to be sure and never to make any mistake about that crucial journey of my life. On his part, my hubby was still struggling financially; he wasn't financially stable yet to take care of himself well enough much more taking up family responsibilities. That was why I encouraged him to

seek greener pastures first before talking about marriage.
While we were waiting for the time to be right, we encountered a lot of challenges. However, change is said to be a constant phenomenon. To prove the agenda and purpose of God in our relationship, after a few months from his travel, he encountered Christ and received a mandate to establish a ministry. That ministry is Divine Light Ministry today.
As God was equipping my man, He was also preparing me to meet his needs. Few months after his ordination, I had a sincere touch and lead of God. I became a born-again Christian. So I went to a pastoral school never with any intention of becoming a pastor but to have a deeper knowledge of God and His Word.
Aside from my conviction from God, I saw in my hubby a passionate man full of wisdom and filled with God's love.
Sometimes, my hubby and I pause to recount our journey together; we reflect on the strange and uncertain encounters we normally have. In the end, we always give God praise for His help and lead.
Below are the most important reasons why I married him:

1. **Communication:** He always ensures that he carries me along in every step of his move. Even when I pretend not to be concerned, he engages me regularly. He wants to

know about everything happening in my life and that makes me love him even more.

2. **Attention:** He pays serious attention to my matter. This is to the extent that every member of my family knows about him. There was a time my younger brother had a police case; my hubby volunteered everything possible till the end of the case.
3. **Care:** He cares so much about me that he usually gives up most of his precious time for mine. Within his financial capacity, he supports me and ensures that I win in most of my targets.

Sometimes, he would travel down to visit me and to ensure that everything is fine with me before he would go back to base.

Communication in marriage plays so much vital role than we can fathom. It is important to open channels for clear and meaningful communication with your spouse so that there is trust and understanding, which means a better relationship between you both.

HOW TO ENSURE A BETTER RELATIONSHIP OR MARRIAGE

1. Try to be specific

Whenever you wish to make a point, make sure you are specific about it. Don't beat around the bush or talk about random and insignificant things. Avoid generalizing by making statements such as "You always say/do this." This may not solve the purpose; instead, you may end up hurting your spouse.

2. Be respectful

No matter what kind of conversation you and your spouse are having, it is important to be respectful towards it. By being a good listener, you show that you respect your partner. When you listen, your partner will do the same if you want to say something.

3. Do not nag or taunt

No one likes getting picked on or nagged. The same holds for your spouse. You cannot keep making your partner guilty or responsible for his past mistakes whenever you wish to make a point. Your partner wants to feel loved and important.

So every time you taunt him or her, it not only causes hurt and pain to him or her, but also affects your relationship. Also, never bring in family members or friends when you have arguments. Always resolve your issues internally.

4. Do not jump to conclusions

Do not assume things or cook up your own stories without having a word with your spouse. For instance, you may get angry that your spouse did not pick up your call without even giving them a chance to explain why it happened. Talk to your spouse about what is bothering you regarding them and know the truth behind their side of the story.

5. Have regular conversations

No matter how busy you are or how much work you have to do, make sure you take out some time in a day to have some meaningful conversation with your spouse. If you cannot think of anything to talk about, get goofy or silly and share some hearty laughs. It is important to communicate with your spouse regularly to keep the love alive in your relationship.

6. No blame games

Even if you are mad because your spouse did something wrong, I do not recommend that you start playing the blame game. Possibly, your spouse might have had self-realization that he made a mistake. He might have been taking necessary measures to make amends. However, even if there are no realizations, it is always better to make a point subtly and politely rather than hitting the other person heavily with all the blames.

7. Express positive feelings

Most of us may talk about our worries, tensions, fears, and other such negative feelings more than we talk about positive feelings such as love, compassion, and humility.

Make sure you include more positive talks, which would include complimenting each other, showing love and care, and other such positive feelings.

I recall the day I finally replied to my husband that I had accepted his marriage proposal. We both were happy as we celebrated God's faithfulness and immediately began to express how much we loved each other. We went ahead to plan on how to better our lives. You should always share positive feelings with your partner.

8. Keep developing yourselves for each other

While we were getting set for marriage, my husband and I kept developing ourselves. I got admission into a higher institution to study my dream course; he was also busy upgrading his business. We were so engaged that we never allowed marriage to interrupt our dreams and aspirations. Dear someone, as you are waiting for your right partner, keep developing yourself. Learn that skill that you are always passionate about; develop it and become a professional at it.

Read more books and keep acquiring basic knowledge that would make you stand tall both in your career and your life generally. It will make you not be desperate about marriage and to be careful while choosing the right spouse.

Beloved reader, before I end it all, let me remind you once

more that there is no perfect relationship or marriage out there. You have to keep molding yours to be better by the day. This is why you both will need a great measure of understanding and tolerance throughout your journey together.

There were times when my hubby and I weren't on good terms. We sometimes disagreed to agree. We had lots of scores and settled them afterward, but we ensured that everything was without involving any third party.

One day, I purposely asked him to give me a break. He complied and never called nor sent me text messages. However, my instruction never lasted up to a month before he hit my phone number again with his call.

"I can't imagine not talking to you or not sharing my issues with you," he said, "Who else will I share it with since you have filled a large vacuum in my heart? I can't do without you, baby; you have become a part of me," he concluded.

Right there, I was just smiling all through the phone call. I felt loved and appreciated; it seemed as if there was an emptiness in me that he had just filled with so much goodness and priceless love.

I am sharing all these with you that you may understand that there is no easy and perfect relationship or marriage. You need to know that you will sometimes feel as if you are tired of being together for too long. You must find the best way to go through such a phase together without hampering your relationship.

There are vital qualities that I also observed in my hubby that helped us build a strong bond in our relationship. The most important of them all is that he has always been supportive of my dreams and aspirations. He believes in me and cannot trade me for anything or anyone else.

With all these qualities of his, I became more intentional about our relationship. That has led us this far up into our marriage.

Dear someone, in the journey of your relationship or marriage, you must be observant and take into consideration these following steps:

- Get into your head

You must have clarity over what exactly your goal is. You cannot get someone you don't want. What do you want? Visualize it in your mind's eye. You must see it clearly if you want to marry someone that aligns with your goals in life.

- Get into your heart

This is where you go from asking yourself what you want to WHY you want it. If you have a very weak WHY, one that is not from your heart, then you will have commitment issues. You will not commit to your intention if you don't even know why you want it in the first place. You must feel it in your heart. Before saying yes to anyone into marriage, ensure that you have answered this question sincerely.

- Get into your hands

Here, you take action on your intention. It is here that you set plans to work on your goals. It's not enough to "manifest" your dream life through the power of affirmation. You cannot have the law of attraction without the action. Even the word "attraction" has "action" in it. To attract, you must take affirmative action. In your relationship or marriage, you must learn to draw your strategies to take positive steps to strengthen your bonds as partners.

When the time was right, my hubby and I got married. Did I tell you about the fact that I rejected so many other suitors with reasons not far-fetched? Some came in the name of marriage but when I gave them a chance to court and prove their intentions, I realized they had other ulterior motives rather than marrying me. Of course, I never wasted any time discarding such persons. For some others, I couldn't visualize their utmost intentions, and when I tabled them before God for better direction, I never received any approval from God that any of them would be my husband. I had to let them go as well.

Finally, you must note that all these strategies, tips, and reasons discussed in this book will only benefit you greatly in your overall relationship or marriage if you walk with God. It should be our number one priority on earth. God is clear about us putting Him first: "But seek ye first the kingdom of God and His righteousness, and all these things shall be added unto you" (Matthew 6:33).

We need to work on doing that before we get a lasting relationship with someone. Won't it be awesome to have someone who loves God more than anything? Your partner wants that from you, too, you know? No matter who you are, I promise that your relationship with God could use some work. Everyone on this planet can improve their relationship with God. This life is a journey. Constantly trying to jump to the next phase of it is just wasting your life if you are not moving in God's direction. It's a gradual process. So is your relationship or marriage; build it gradually with God as its pillar! How? Talk to him always in prayer.

CHAPTER EIGHT

PRAYERS FOR MARITAL BREAKTHROUGH

O thou that hearest prayer, unto thee shall all flesh come (Psalms 65:2).

Are you a single brother or sister? Are you waiting upon God for your own marital breakthrough?

Have you been a victim of numerous disappointments and broken marital promises? If your answer to any of these questions is yes, then these prayer points are for you.

Through the power of prayers, every believer can turn any tide to their favor. Enough is enough for that marital delay. It is the perfect will of God for a man or woman who desires to be married to be married to their God-ordained spouse. These night prayers will empower you to secure your marital destiny through the fire of prayers.

Child of God, the devil is a wicked fellow; he will do everything to ensure that your life remains stagnant and that you continue to shed tears over numerous marital failures. But you must rise up to resist him alongside all his wicked snares. Pray the devil out of your life and your marital destiny.

In Luke 18:1, Jesus tells us to pray always. It's only through the power of prayers that we all can overcome all the forces of darkness fighting against our marital destinies. Therefore, I encourage you today to engage in these prayers against marital delay in your life with violent faith and holy anger. Let the devil know that you can't stand his excesses in your life any more. Pray with a desperate faith and give God no option but to answer you speedily.

I declare to you this day that within the next 7 days of your saying these prayers fervently, you shall be connected to your God-ordained spouse in Jesus' name. And for those who are going through the toughest times in their relationships or marriages, you will experience divine breakthrough in no time.

PRAYERS

Prayer of Thanksgiving

Appreciate God for his Love, mercy and protection that you have been enjoying. Thank him for how far he has brought you as at this point.

Praise and Worship

- thou that troubleth my Israel (insert your name), my God shall trouble you today in the name of Jesus.
- Thou rain of blessing, fall upon my marital destiny in the name of Jesus.
- Magnets of favor, rain upon my marital destiny in the name of Jesus.

- Every Power of spiritual dowry working against my life die in the name of Jesus.
- Lord, let divine beauty settle upon my life in the name of Jesus.
- Blood of Jesus, speak freedom into my marital destiny in the name of Jesus.
- Angels of the living God, go into the coven of enchanters, and retrieve my stolen wedding gown/suit in the name of Jesus.
- Every good thing in my marital destiny that I have lost to the devil, I recover you by fire in the name of Jesus.
- By the power in the blood of Jesus, I set myself free from evil character discouraging my divine partner in Jesus' name.
- Heavens over my marital breakthrough, open by fire in the name of Jesus.

Prayer for Family Unity

Gracious and Most Holy Father, a house cannot function if its members are not on the same page. How can we all work together unless we agree? Therefore, living in unity helps us to come together for our common goal.

- Give us all love and compassion for one another, so that this family may serve as a great example for others. Let our spiritual life flourish, that our bonds may grow tighter in You in Jesus' name. Amen!

- Every power fighting against the peace of my home, I cause you destruction and death in mighty name of Jesus. Amen.
- Every serpentine spirit causing misunderstanding and war in my home, be destroyed and end your operation in the mighty name of Jesus. Amen.

www.ingramcontent.com/pod-product-compliance
Lightning Source LLC
LaVergne TN
LVHW012114160826
845678LV00014B/3089

* 9 7 9 8 8 4 8 0 3 2 1 9 2 *